WORKING PAPERS
VOLUME I: CHAPTERS 1-14
TO ACCOMPANY

INTERMEDIATE ACCOUNTING

Eighth Edition

Donald E. Kieso, PH.D., C.P.A.

KPMG Peat Marwick Emeritus Professor of Accounting
Northern Illinois University
DeKalb, Illinois

Jerry J. Weygandt, PH.D., C.P.A.

Arthur Andersen Alumni Professor of Accounting
University of Wisconsin
Madison, Wisconsin

John Wiley & Sons, Inc.
New York • Chichester • Brisbane • Toronto • Singapore

ISBN 0-471-01389-7

10 9 8 7 6 5 4 3

		General Journal			1 Debit	2 Credit

Name

Section

Date

Digable Planets Hardware Store

		1	2
	General Journal	Debit	Credit
(a)			

	General Journal		1 Debit	2 Credit
(a) Cont.				
(b)	Digable Planets Hardware Store			
	Income Statement (Partial)			
	For the Month Ended May 31, 1996			

		Ella Fitzgerald Company		1 Debit	2 Credit
		Trial Balance			
		April 30, 1995			

Exercise 3-4

Sons of Soul Corporation

				Debit	Credit
		Sons of Soul Corporation			
		Trial Balance (corrected)			
		April 30			

				1	2
		Jimmie Gilmore Co.			
		Trial Balance		Debit	Credit
		June 30, 1996			

Exercise 3-6

Right Way Computer Services

		General Journal		Debit	Credit

Shana Alexander Company

(a)		General Journal		1 Debit	2 Credit

(b)					

Name

Section

Date

Reno, Inc.

	General Journal		Debit	Credit
		1		2

Exercise 3-9

(a)	General Journal			**Susan Powter Resort**

	General Journal		1 Debit	2 Credit
(a)	continued			
(b)	**Susan Powter Resort**			
	Adjusted Trial Balance			
	August 31, 1995			

Section

Date   **Holyfield Company**

(a)	General Journal		1 Debit	2 Credit

Exercise 3-11

(a)	General Journal			**Mitch Williams Inc.**

Mitch Williams Inc.

	General Journal		1 Debit	2 Credit
(b)				

Exercise 3-12

	General Journal		1 Debit	2 Credit
(a)				
(b)				
(c)				
(d)				

			1	2
(e)				
(f)				
(g)				
(h)				
(i)				

Cracker Jax Women's Wear

(a)

Cost of Goods Sold
Ledger Account

Debit

Credit

(b)

Cracker Jax Women's Wear

Cost of Goods Sold Section

(c)

		1	2
(a)			
(b)			

Hannah Corporation

		1	2
(a)			
(b)			

Exercise 3-16

Fleiss Co., Inc.

		1	2
(a)			
(b)			

Name

Section

Date

Fleiss Co., Inc.

General Ledger Accounts

(c)&(e)

(d) | General Journal | Debit | Credit

	General Journal		1 Debit	2 Credit

Mandela Co.
Work Sheet (Partial)
For the Month Ended April 30, 1995

	Account Title	1 Adjusted Trial Balance Dr.	2 Adjusted Trial Balance Cr.	3 Income Statement Dr.	4 Income Statement Cr.	5 Balance Sheet Dr.	6 Balance Sheet Cr.

		Mandela Co. Balance Sheet April 30, 1995		1 Debit	2 Credit

DeKlerk Co.
Work Sheet (Partial)
For the Month Ended February 28, 1996

	1	2	3	4	5	6	7	8
	Trial Balance		Adjustments		Adjusted Trial Balance		Income Statement	
Account Titles	Debit	Credit	Debit	Credit	Debit	Credit	Debit	Credit

Section

Date   **Scratch Miniature Golf and Driving Range Inc.**

			1	2
			Debit	Credit

Section

Date   **Chita Rivera Company**

		1	2

Exercise 3-23

Bonnie Miller, M.D.

Bonnie Miller, M.D.

Conversion of Cash Basis to Accrual Basis

For the Year 1995

		1	2

Exercise 3-25

Hal Ketchum Corp.

Hal Ketchum Corp.

Income Statement (Cash Basis)

For the Year Ended December 31

Hal Ketchum Corp.

Income Statement (Accrual Basis)

For the Year Ended December 31

Section

Date

Excalibur Company

Exercise 3-27

General Ledger Account				**Bertie Wooster Company**		
(a)&(b)		Debit				Credit

Bertie Wooster Company

			1	2
(c)		**Bertie Wooster Company** Schedule of Creditors — As of September 30		

Exercise 3-28

Fink-Nottle Company

(a) Journal	(b) Columns

Section ________________________

Date ________________________   **Laura Spencer, D.D.S.**

General Ledger Accounts

(a)&(d)		Debit			Credit

Name

Section

Date

Laura Spencer, D.D.S.

General Ledger Accounts

(a)&(d)		Debit			Credit

	1	2
Laura Spencer, D.D.S. Trial Balance Before Closing (b) September 30	Debit	Credit

Laura Spencer, D.D.S.

Income Statement

For the Month of September

			1	2

Laura Spencer, D.D.S.

Balance Sheet

(c) September 30

Laura Spencer, D.D.S.

Statement of Capital

For the Month of September

(e) **Laura Spencer, D.D.S.**

Post-closing Trial Balance

September 30

	Debit	Credit

General Ledger Accounts

(a),(b)&(d)		Debit			Credit

Name

Section

Date

Young & Restless Company

General Ledger Accounts

		Debit			Credit

Name

Section

Date

Young & Restless Company

General Ledger Accounts

	Debit		Credit

Name

Section

Date

Young & Restless Company

(c)	**Young & Restless Company** Adjusted Trial Balance January 31, 1996		Debit (1)	Credit (2)

	1	2
(e) **Young & Restless Company** Income Statement For the Month of January 1996		

	Debit	Credit
(f) **Young & Restless Company** Trial Balance After Closing January 31, 1996		

		1	2
(e)	**Young & Restless Company** Balance Sheet As of January 31, 1996		

Name

Section

Date   **Wolftrap Theater**

	General Journal	1 Debit	2 Credit
(a)			
(b)			

Name

Section

Date

Laura Santoro

(a)	General Journal		1 Debit	2 Credit

(b)	**Laura Santoro, Consulting Engineer** Income Statement For the Year Ended December 31, 1995		1 Debit	2 Credit

Section

Date   **Laura Santoro**

(b)

Laura Santoro, Consulting Engineer

Balance Sheet

For the Year Ended December 31, 1995

Laura Santoro, Consulting Engineer

Statement of Owner's Equity

For the Year Ended December 31, 1995

Nava Advertising Corporation

General Ledger Accounts

(a)

	Debit		Credit

		1	2
(b)	**Nava Advertising Corporation** Income Statement For the Year Ended December 31, 1996		

		1	2
	Nava Advertising Corporation Statement of Retained Earnings For the Year Ended December 31, 1996		

Name

Section

Date

Nava Advertising Corporation

	1	2
Nava Advertising Corporation		
Balance Sheet		
(b) Continued — December 31, 1996		

(c)

Name

Section

Date

Nicole Thompson, Realtor

(a)	General Journal		Debit		Credit	

Name

Section

Date

Nicole Thompson, Realtor

(a) Continued	General Journal		1 Debit	2 Credit

Kishwaukee Golf Club, Inc.

General Ledger Accounts

(a),(b)&(d)

Name

Section

Date

Kishwaukee Golf Club, Inc.

General Ledger Accounts

Name

Section

Date

Kishwaukee Golf Club, Inc.

General Ledger Accounts

General Ledger Accounts

Section

Date   **Kishwaukee Golf Club, Inc.**

(b)	General Journal		1 Debit	2 Credit

Name

Section

Date

Kishwaukee Golf Club, Inc.

Trial Balances

(c),(f)	Account Titles	Second Trial Balance		Third Trial Balance	
		Debit	Credit	Debit	Credit

		General Journal			1 Debit	2 Credit
(d)						
(e)						

Name

Section

Date

Madonna Boutique

General Ledger Accounts

(a)

Section

Date

Madonna Boutique

General Ledger Accounts

General Ledger Accounts

Name

Section

Date

Madonna Boutique

General Ledger Accounts

(b)	General Journal		1 Debit	2 Credit
	Adjusting Entries			

Madonna Boutique

		1	2
(c)	General Journal	Debit	Credit
	Closing Entries		

(a)	General Journal		Debit	Credit

General Ledger Accounts

(b),(d)&(g)		Debit			Credit

Mattie Gibbs Company

General Ledger Accounts

(b),(d)&(g)		Debit			Credit

Name

Section

Date

Mattie Gibbs Company

General Ledger Accounts

(b),(d)&(g)		Debit			Credit

			1	2
(c)	**Mattie Gibbs Company** Trial Balance 1/31/96		Debit	Credit

| (d) | Adjusting entries |

Name

Section

Date

Mattie Gibbs Company

(e)		**Mattie Gibbs Company** Adjusted Trial Balance 1/31/96		1 Debit	2 Credit

Mattie Gibbs Company

			1	2
(f)	**Mattie Gibbs Company** Income Statement January, 1996			

Name

Section

Date

Mattie Gibbs Company

		Mattie Gibbs Company Balance Sheet January, 1996		1	2
(f)					

Name

Section

Date

Mattie Gibbs Company

(g)	Closing Entries		1 Debit	2 Credit

(h)	**Mattie Gibbs Company**		Debit	Credit
	Post-closing Trial Balance			
	1/31/96			

(a)	General Journal		Debit	Credit
			1	2

(b)				

Name

Section

Date

Boffo Company

		General Journal			1 Debit	2 Credit
(a)						
(d)		Estimated inventory, January 31, 1995, computation:				

Name

Section

Date

Boffo Company

Boffo Company
Balance Sheet
As of January 31, 1995

			1	2
(f)				

			1	2
	Boffo Company			
	Income Statement			
	For the Month of January 1995			
(f)				

Boffo Company

Statement of Retained Earnings

For the Month of January, 1995

Name

Section

Date

Brendan Noble

		General Journal		1 Debit	2 Credit
(b)					

			1		2
	Brendan Noble Income Statement For the Year Ended December 31, 1996				
(d)					

Name

Section

Date

Brendan Noble

		Brendan Noble Balance Sheet As of December 31, 1996	1	2
(d)				

		1	2
	Brendan Noble Statement of Capital For the Year Ended December 31, 1996		
(d)			
(e)	General Journal	Debit	Credit

Farmers Laundromat Inc.

		1	2
(a)		Debit	Credit

Farmers Laundromat Inc.

				1	2	3
(b)						

Farmers Laundromat Inc.

		1	2
(c)	**Farmers Laundromat Inc.** Trial Balance September 30, 1996		

(c)

			1	2
(a)	**Micromash Sales and Service** Income Statement For the Year Ended January 31, 1996			
			Cash Basis	Accrual Basis
(b)	**Micromash Sales and Service** Balance Sheet As of January 31, 1996			
			Cash Basis	Accrual Basis

	1	2
(c)		

Name

Section

Date

Basler Specialty Shops
Worksheet to Convert Trial Balance to Accrual Basis
December 31, 1996

(a)	Account Title	Cash Basis		Adjustments		Accrual Basis	
		1 Dr.	2 Cr.	3 Dr.	4 Cr.	5 Dr.	6 Cr.

Section

Date   **Basler Specialty Shops**

Basler Specialty Shops

			1	2
(b)	Basler Specialty Shops Statement of Changes in Shirley Basler, Capital For the Year Ended December 31, 1996			

Section ____

Date ____   **Guiding Light Company**

General Ledger Accounts

(a)&(c)	(allow 2 lines per account except Accts. Pay.–allow 5)									

General Ledger Accounts

Name

Section

Date

Guiding Light Company

(b)	General Journal		1 Debit	2 Credit

Name

Section

Date

Special Journals

Sales Journal		17				
Cash Receipts Journal		43				
Purchases Journal		8				
Cash Payments Journal		44				

Name

Section

Date

Name

Section

Date

Mel Gibson Furniture Co.

Exercise 4-2

Angelica Houston Video Company

	Jan. 1, 1996	Dec. 31, 1996	Change

Meg Ryan Products Co.

			1	2
(a)				
(b)				
(c)				

Meg Ryan Products Co.

		1	2
(d)			

Exercise 4-4

Richard Chamberlain Inc.

Richard Chamberlain Inc.

Income Statement

For the Year Ended December 31, 1996

			1	2	3
		Far and Away Company			
		Income Statement			
		For the Year Ended December 31, 1996			
(a)					

			1	**2**
	Far and Away Company			
	Income Statement			
	For the Year Ended December 31, 1996			
(b)				

(c)	

		Harrison Ford Corp. Income Statement For the Year Ended Dec. 31, 1996	1	2	3	4

			1	2	3	4
(a)		**Clint Eastwood Inc.** Income Statement For the Year Ended Dec. 31, 1996				

		Clint Eastwood Inc. Income Statement For the Year Ended December 31, 1996	1	2
(b)				
(c)				

			1	2	3
(a)	**Emma Thompson Shoe Co.** Income Statement For the Year Ended December 31, 1996				

Emma Thompson Shoe Co.

		1	2
(b)	**Emma Thompson Shoe Co.** Income Statement For the Year Ended December 31, 1996		

(c)

Emma Thompson Shoe Co.

		Kenneth Branagh Corporation Income Statement For the Year Ended December 31, 1996			1	2	3
(a)							

		1	2
(b)	**Kenneth Branagh Corporation** Income Statement For the Year Ended December 31, 1996		

(c)

Anthony Hopkins Co.

		Anthony Hopkins Co.		1	2
		Combined Statement of Income and Retained Earnings			
		For the Year Ended December 31, 1996			

Julia Roberts Inc.

Income Statement

For the Year Ended December 31, 1996

(a)

		1	2
(b)	**Julia Roberts Inc.** Combined Statement of Income and Retained Earnings For the Year Ended December 31, 1996		

(c)

	1	2
Tom Hanks Corp.		
Income Statement		
(a) For the Year Ended December 31, 1996		

	1	2
Tom Hanks Corp.		
(b) Statement of Retained Earnings		
For the Year Ended December 31, 1996		

Bette Midler Corporation

		1	2

			1	2
	Sean Connery Corporation			
	Income Statement			
	For the Year Ended December 31, 1996			
(a)				
	Supporting Computations:			

				1	2
(a)		**Michael J. Fox Corporation** Statement of Retained Earnings For the Year Ended December 31, 1996			

Exercise 4-16

Denzel Washington Corporation

Denzel Washington Corporation

Exercise 4-17

Charles Grodin Inc.

(a)

(b)

(c)

(d)

Section

Date   **Doubtfire Inc.**

General Journal.		Debit	Credit
		1	2

Note XX:

Computations:

			1	2
	Liam Neeson Company			
	Combined Statement of Income and Retained Earnings			
	For the Year Ended December 31, 1996			

Mariah Carey Corporation

		1	2
Mariah Carey Corporation			
Combined Statement of Income and Retained Earnings			
For the Year Ended December 31, 1996			

		Aerosmith Inc. Income Statement (Partial) For the Year Ended December 31, 1996		1	2

		Reba McEntire Corporation Combined Statement of Income and Retained Earnings For the Year Ended June 30, 1996	1	2	3	4
(a)						

Section

Date

Reba McEntire Corporation

(a)	Continued	1	2	3	4

Reba McEntire Corporation

			1	2
(b)		**Reba McEntire Corporation** Combined Statement of Income and Retained Earnings For the Year Ended June 30, 1996		

(a)	**Pearl Jam Corporation** Combined Statement of Income and Retained Earnings For the Year Ended December 31, 1996	1	2	3	4

| | 1 | 2 | 3 | 4 |

Pearl Jam Corporation
Statement of Income and Retained Earnings
For the Year Ended December 31, 1996

(b)

1.

2.

3.

4.

		1	2

(a)

Clay Walker Corp.

Statement of Retained Earnings

For the Year Ended December 31, 1996

(b)

				1	2
(Situation A)	**Wynonna Company**				
	Combined Statement of Income and Retained Earnings				
	For the Year Ended December 31, 1996				

Name

Section

Date

Wynonna Company

			1		2
(Situation B)	**Wynonna Company**				
	Combined Statement of Income and Retained Earnings				
	For the Year Ended December 31, 1996				

	(Situation C)			1		2
	Wynonna Company					
	Combined Statement of Income and Retained Earnings					
	For the Year Ended December 31, 1996					

			1	2
		Carlito Corporation Income Statement For the Year Ended December 31, 1996		

(a)

(b)

(c)

Date   **Georgia-Pacific Corporation**

1.

2.

3.

Name

Section

Date

Georgia-Pacific Corporation

4.

5.

Georgia-Pacific Corporation

Name

Section

Date

Exercise 5-3

Belva Lockwood Enterprises

			1	2
		Gertrude Stein Inc. Balance Sheet December 31, 19—		
		Assets		
		Liabilities and Stockholders' Equity		

Gertrude Stein Inc.

		1	2
Liabilities and Stockholders' Equity (continued)			

Celia Cruz Company

			1	2	3
Celia Cruz Company					
Balance Sheet					
December 31, 1996					
Assets					

Celia Cruz Company

		1	2	3
Liabilities and Stockholders' Equity				

Section

Date   **Angeles Ochoa Company**

Angeles Ochoa Company

Balance Sheet

July 31, 1996

Assets

Liabilities and Stockholders' Equity

Exercise 5-7

Rico Company

		1	2

Exercise 5-8

Natalie Cole Corporation

Kathleen Battle Sound Machines

	General Journal		1 Debit	2 Credit

(b)

Exercise 5-10

Otis Clay Corporation

Section

Date   **Oliver Cromwell Company**

		1	2
	Oliver Cromwell Company		
	Partial Balance Sheet		
	As of December 31, 1996		
(a)			
(b)			

Exercise 5-13

Exercise 5-14

Henry Tudor Inc.

Henry Tudor Inc.

Statement of Cash Flows

For the Year Ended December 31, 1996

Catherine Aragon Corporation

Catherine Aragon Corporation

Statement of Cash Flows

For the Year Ended December 31, 1996

1 2

Anne Boleyn Corporation

			Anne Boleyn Corporation		1	2
			Statement of Cash Flows			
			For the Year Ended December 31, 1996			

			1	2	3
	Jane Seymour Corporation Balance Sheet December 31, 1996				
	Assets				

			1	2	3
	Liabilities and Stockholders' Equity				

		Thomas More Corporation Statement of Cash Flows For the Year Ended December 31, 1996		1	2

					1		2

Thomas More Corporation

Balance Sheet

At December 31, 1996

Assets

Liabilities and Stockholders' Equity

Balance Sheet

As of End of Fiscal Year

				1		2	
	Balance Sheet (Continued)						

Section ____

Date ____   **Santana, Inc.**

		Santana, Inc. Balance Sheet December 31, 1996	1	2	3	4

Balance Sheet (Continued)

		1	2	3	4

		U2 Company Balance Sheet As of December 31, 1996	1	2	3	4

Name

Section

Date

U2 Company

		1	2	3	4
Balance Sheet (Continued)					

Section

Date   **Run-D.M.C. Corporation**

		1	2	3	4
Run-D.M.C. Corporation Balance Sheet As of December 31, 1996					

Run-D.M.C. Corporation

		1	2	3	4
Balance Sheet (Continued)					

		1	2	3	4
	John Lennon Corporation Balance Sheet As of December 31, 1996				

Name

Section

Date

John Lennon Corporation

		1	2	3	4
Balance Sheet (Continued)					

			1	2	3	4
(a)	**Tracy Chapman Inc.** Statement of Cash Flows For the Year Ended December 31, 1996					

Section

Date

Tracy Chapman Inc.

		1	2
(b)	**Tracy Chapman Inc.** Balance Sheet December 31, 1996		

(c)

Section

Date   **B & B Inc.**

(a)

B & B Inc.

Income Statement

For the Five Months Ended May 31, 1996

			1	2	3	4
(b)		**B & B Inc.** Balance Sheet May 31, 1996				

(a)

(b)

(c)

(d)

(e)

Name

Section

Date

Name

Section

Date

Name

Section

Date

1. a.
   b.
   c.

2. a.
   b.
   c.

Exercise 6-2

Kriss Kross

a.

b.

c.

Exercise 6-3

a.

b.

c.

d.

(a)

(b)

(c)

(d)

Exercise 6-5

(a)

(b)

(c)

(a)

(b)

(c)

Exercise 6-7

(a)

(b)

(c)

Exercise 6-8

David Bowie

(a)

(b)

(a)

(b)

Exercise 6-10

Posies Inc.

Building A:

Building B:

Building C:

Recommendation:

Exercise 6-11

Dianna Ross

Exercise 6-12

Leith Chrysalis

Ned's Atomic Dustbin, Inc.

Exercise 6-14

Erasure, Inc.

(i)

(ii)

Exercise 6-16

Pixies, Inc.

Exercise 6-17

Robyn Hitchcock Leasing Company

Immediate Payment:

Annual Payments:

Recommendation:

Exercise 6-19

Immediate Payment:

Annual Payments:

Recommendation:

Whitney Houston

Exercise 6-21

Julia Roberts

Exercise 6-22

Cindy Crawford

1.

2.

3.

Name

Section

Date

4.

5.

(a)

(b)

(c)

(d)

Name

Section

Date

Mack Aroni

		1	2

R.L. Stein Inc.

			1	2

Bid A:

Bid B:

(a)

(b)

(c)

(a)

(b)

(c)

(d)

Recommended option:

Section

Date

(a)

(b)

(c)

Section ____

Date ____ **Georgia O'Keefe**

	1	2	3	4
Present Value of $1 for Time Periods at 12% Interest Rate (Table 6-4)				
Periods		Cumulative		Increment
1-5				
6-10				
11-30				
31-40				
Present Value of Cash Receipts and Payments for Cher's Vineyard				
Years	Receipts	Expenditures		PV at 12%
1-5				
6-10				
11-30				
31-40				
Present Value of future net cash inflows				
Conclusion:				

1.

2.

3.

4.

Vendor A:

Vendor B:

Vendor C:

1.

2.

3.

El Greco Company

Section

Date   **Miró Inc.**

		1	2
1.			
2.	Project I		
	Project II		

			1	2
3.	Bonus Plan			
	Pension Plan			

Alexander Calder, Inc.

Purchase

Leasee

(a)

(b)

(c)

Name

Section

Date

Name

Section

Date

Name

Section

Date

Name

Section

Date

(a)

(b)

Section

Date

1.

2.

3.

4.

5.

			1	2
			Debit	Credit

Exercise 7-4

Montgomery's Auto Repair Service

Section

Date   **Acadian Company**

(a)

Acadian Company

Bank Reconciliation

July 31

		1	2

(b)

		Debit	Credit

			1	2
(a)	**Monie Love Company** Bank Reconciliation August 31, 1995			
(b)			Debit	Credit
(c)				

Leontine Price Company

		1	2	3

Exercise 7-8

Bala Bautista

		1	2	3

Section

Date   **Igneous Company**

		1	2
(a)		Debit	Credit
(b)			

Sunchi Company

		1	2

Exercise 7-11

G. Washington Inc.

		Debit	Credit
(a)			
(b)			

Exercise 7-12

J. Adams Corporation

(a)			
(b)			

Exercise 7-13

Amy Liu, Inc.

		1	2

Exercise 7-14

Madison Corp.

		Debit	Credit

		General Journal		1 Debit	2 Credit

	General Journal		Debit	Credit

Exercise 7-17

Monteray Inc.

			Debit	Credit
(a)				
(b)				

William Henry Corporation

	1	2
(a)		

(b)

		Debit	Credit

(c)

Tyler Corp.

		Debit	Credit
(a)			

(b)

	1	2

			1	2
			Debit	Credit
1.				
2.				

Fillmore Company

		1	2
		Debit	Credit
(a)			

Schedule of Note Discount Amortization

Date	Amortization	Present Value of Note

| (c) | | | |

Section

Date

			1	2

(a)

			Debit	Credit

(b)

Section

Date

		1	2
1.			
2.			
3.			
4.			
5.			

Section

Date   **Larry King Equipment Co.**

		General Journal	1 Debit	2 Credit
(a)				

			Per Balance Sheet	After Adjustment
(b)				

Section

Date   **Dr. Quinn Co.**

Dr. Quinn Co.

Bank Reconciliation

June 30, 1995

(a)

(b)

Doug Inc.

			1	2
	Doug Inc. Bank Reconciliation November 30, 1995			
(a)				
(b)				

		1	2
	Computation of Cash Balance Per Books – General Checking Account		
(a)			

Clarissa Industries

Bank Reconciliation–General Checking Account

June 30, 1995

1.

2.

3.

4.

5.

Whoopi Goldberg Corporation

		1	2
(a)			
(b)			
(c)			

		1	2
(a)			

(a)

Schedule 1

Aging Schedule

(b)

Name

Section

Date

Paul Newman Inc.

		General Journal		1 Debit	2 Credit

Corrected

Aging Schedule

Section ____________________________

Date ______________________________   **Jane Seymour Company**

		General Journal		1 Debit	2 Credit
(1)					
(2)					
(3)					
(4)					
(5)					
(6)					

Jane Seymour Company

Section

Date   **Bruce Willis Company**

		General Journal		Debit	Credit
(a)					
(b)					

Problem 7-12

Bo Jackson Sports Company

	General Journal		Debit	Credit
			1	2

Schedule of Note Discount Amortization

Name

Section

Date

La Tourette Inc.

		General Journal		1 Debit	2 Credit
(a)					
(b)					

Schedule of Discount Amortization

Name

Section

Date

La Tourette Inc.

		General Journal		Debit [1]	Credit [2]
(c)					
(d)					
(e)					

(a)

(b)

(c)

(a)	Ritter Supply Accounts Receivable Aging Schedule November 30, 1995		1	2	3

(b)

(c)

(d)

B. Hoger Machinery Co.

(a)

(b)

(c)

	1	2
(a) **Weaver, Inc.** Long-Term Receivables Section of Balance Sheet December 31, 1996		

	1	2
(b) **Weaver, Inc.** Selected Balance Sheet Balances December 31, 1996		

			1	2
(c)		**Weaver, Inc.**		
		Interest Revenue from Long-Term Receivables		
		And Gains Recognized on Sale of Assets		
		For Year Ended December 31, 1996		
		Computations:		

Lilja, Inc.

			1	2	3	4
		Lilja, Inc. Bank Reconciliation For the Month of December, 1995	11/30/95	Receipts	Disbursements	12/31/95

		Lilja, Inc. Bank Reconciliation For the Month of December, 1995	1 11/30/95	2 Receipts	3 Disbursements	4 12/31/95
(a)						
(b)						

(a)	**Montana Division—** **Mark Kaleel Manufacturing Company** Bank Reconciliation For the Month of August, 1996	1 7/31/96	2 Receipts	3 Disbursements	4 8/31/96

Name

Section

Date

Mark Kaleel Manufacturing Company

			1	2	3	4
(b)		**Montana Division—** **Mark Kaleel Manufacturing Company** Bank Reconciliation For the Month of August, 1996	7/31/96	Receipts	Disbursements	8/31/96

			Hrubec Corp.						Waubonsee Factors, Inc.		
			Debit	Credit					Debit	Credit	

			1	2
(b)				
(c)				

Name

Section

Date

Frippery Furnishings, Inc.

	General Journal		1 Debit	2 Credit
(a)				

Frippery Furnishings, Inc.

		1	2
(b)			

		General Journal		1 Debit	2 Credit
(a)					
(b)					

Name

Section

Date

Green Mountain Woolens, Inc.

General Journal		1 Debit	2 Credit

(a)

(b)

Name

Section

Date

Georgia Pacific Corporation

Name

Section

Date

Exercise 8-2

Muddy Waters Company

Exercise 8-4

Junior Kimbrough

Machine Company

General Journal		Debit	Credit

Name

Section

Date

R. L. Burnside Company

Transaction	1 Purchase & Payable Should Be Recognized in	2 Purchase & Payable Were Recognized in	3 Correcting Journal Entries Needed	4	5 Should Inventory Be Included in Ending Inventory?	6 Was Inventory Included in Ending Inventory?	7 Dollar Adjustments Needed

			1	2	3
(a)					
(b)					
(c)					
(d)					

Section

Date   **Leno Corporation**

		General Journal			1 Debit	2 Credit

		General Journal		1 Debit	2 Credit
(a)					
(b)					

		1	2
(a)			
(b)			

			1		2
			Debit		Credit
(c)					
(d)					

Exercise 8-11

Chevy Chase Company

1.	Current Year	Subsequent Year
Working Capital	Overstated	No effect

2.

3.

Exercise 8-12

Clive James Company

(a)

(b)

(c)

Event	Effect of Error	Adjust Income

Exercise 8-14

Joan Rivers Company

	Year	1 Net Income Per Books	2 Add Overstate- ment Jan. 1	3 Deduct Understate- ment Jan. 1	4 Deduct Overstate- ment Dec. 31	5 Add Understate- ment Dec. 31	6 Corrected Net Income

	1	2
Cost of Goods Sold	**Ending Inventory**	

(a)

  1.

  2.

(b)

(c)

(d)

(a) (1)

  (2)

(b) (1)

  (2)

(c)

(d) Conclusion:

			1	2	3
(a)	**A.C.Neher Company**				
	Computation of Inventory				
	FIFO Inventory Method				
	March 31, 1995				
			Units	Unit Cost	Total Cost

			1	2	3
(b)	**A.C. Neher Company**				
	Computation of Inventory				
	LIFO Inventory Method				
	March 31, 1995				
			Units	Unit Cost	Total Cost

			1	2	3
(c)	**A.C. Neher Company**				
	Computation of Inventory				
	Weighted Average Inventory Method				
	March 31, 1995				
			Units	Unit Cost	Total Cost

(a) 1.

2.

3.

(b) 1.

2.

Exercise 8-19

Kaster Company

(a) 1.   2.

(b) 1.   2.

Burke Corporation

Trial Balances

		1	2	3	4
		First-in, First-out		Last-in, First-out	

Exercise 8-21

Gleason Corporation

Schedules of Cost of Goods Sold

For the First Quarter Ended March 31, 1996

Gleason Corporation

	FIFO	LIFO

Schedules Computing Ending Inventory

(a)

(b)

(c)

Exercise 8-23

Mario Lemieux Inc.

(a)

(b)

		1	2	3	4	5	6
			Material X	Material Y	Total Cost	Total Unit	Unit Cost

(c)

Brett Hull Corporation

		1 No. Units	2 Unit Cost	3 Total Cost
(a)	(1)			
	(2)			
	(3)			
	(4)			
(b)				

Stan Mitira Company

(a)

Exercise 8-26

Bobby Orr Corp.

(b)

(c)

Wayne Gretzky Company

Exercise 8-29

Casey Stengel Ltd.

Name

Section

Date

			1		2	

Name

Section

Date

		1	2

Section

Date   **Fats Domino Company**

	Schedule of Adjustments	1	2	3
		Inventory	Accounts Payable	Net Sales

	1	2	3
Schedule of Adjustments	Inventory	Accounts Payable	Sales

Name ____ Problem 8-4

Section ____

Date ____ **Conway Twitty Company**

		General Journal		Debit	Credit
				1	2
(a)	1.				
	2.				

	General Journal		Debit	Credit
(b) 1.				
2.				
3.				

(c)

Section ____

Date ____   **Dolly Parton Company**

		1 Date	2 No. Units	3 Unit Cost	4 Total Cost
(a) 1.	First-in, First-out				
2.	Last-in, First-out				
3.	Average Cost				

			1	2	3	4	5	6
(b) 1.	First-in, First-out		Purchased		Sold		Balance	
			No. of Units	Unit Cost	No. of Units	Unit Cost	No. of Units	Unit Cost
2.	Last-in, First-out							

Name

Section

Date

Dolly Parton Company

		Purchased		Sold		Balance	
		1	2	3	4	5	6
		No. of Units	Unit Cost	No. of Units	Unit Cost	No. of Units	Unit Cost
3.	Average Cost						

Section

Date   **Randy Travis Inc.**

		Date	No. Units	Unit Cost	Total Cost
(a) 1.	First-in, First-out				
2.	Last-in, First-out				
3.	Average Cost				

(b)

		1	2	3	4	5	6
(a) 1.	First-in, First-out	Quarter	Sales	Ending Inventory	Purchases	Beginning Inventory	Gross Profit

		1	2	3	4	5	6
2.	Last-in, First-out						

Name

Section

Date

Connie Francis Company

3.	Average Cost	1 Quarter	2 Sales	3 Ending Inventory	4 Purchases	5 Beginning Inventory	6 Gross Profit

(b)

		1	2	3	4
		FIFO	LIFO	Weighted Average Cost	
	Computation of Cost of Goods Sold				
	Computation of Ending Inventory				

Jan & Dean Company

(a)

(b)

(c)

(d)

(e)

(f)

Section

Date   **Oscar Wilde Company**

		1	2
Accounts Affected:			
Calculations for 1996 and 1997		1996	1997
Income			
Cost of Goods Sold and Ending Inventory			

Oscar Wilde Company

			1	2
	Calculations continued:		1996	1997
	Determination of Cash			
	Determination of Retained Earnings			

(a)

(b)

Dr. Seuss Inc.

		Effect on Income Before Income Taxes— Change from FIFO to LIFO Inventory Method For the Year Ended December 31, 1997		1	2

			1	2	3
(a)		**Edith Sitwell Wholesalers Inc.**			
		Computation of Internal Conversion Price Index			
			December 31, 1995		December 31, 1996
(b)		**Edith Sitwell Wholesalers Inc.**			
		Computation of Inventory Amounts			
			Current Inventory at Base Cost	Conversion Price Index	Inventory at LIFO Cost
		December 31, 1995			
		December 31, 1996			

Name

Section

Date

	1 Base Year Cost	2 Index	3 Dollar Value LIFO	4
December 31, 1994				
December 31, 1995				
December 31, 1996				

Thomas Hardy Corp.

	Explanation		1		2 Physical Inventory		3 General Ledger Control Acct.		4 Tabulating Departments Inventory Detail
	Balance Per Client				401200		466900		465100
	Adjusted Balance								

(a)

			1	2	3	4	5	6
(b)				1993	1992	1991	1990	1989

Name

Section

Date

Name

Section

Date

Section

Date

Name

Section

Date

	Part No.	1 Quantity	Per Unit 2 Cost	3 Market	4 Total Cost	5 Total Market	6 Lower of Cost or Market

Exercise 9-2

N. Kerrigan Company

Item	Ceiling	Floor	Replacement Cost	Market	Designated Cost	LCM

Name

Section

Date

Sonja Henie Company

1	2	3	4	5	6	7	8
Item No.	Cost Per Unit	Replacement Cost	Net Realizable Value	NRV Less Normal Profit	Designated Market Value	Quantity	Final Inventory Value

		1	2
		Debit	Credit
(a)			
(b)			
(c)			

Bonnie Blair Enterprises

		1	2	3
		February	March	April
(a)				
(b)			Debit	Credit

Corbett Realty Corporation

	1 No. of Lots	2 Price per Lot	3 Total Selling Price	4 Relative Sales Price	5 Total Cost	6 Cost Allocated	7 Cost per Lot	8
Group 1								
Group 2								
Group 3								
	Units Sold	Unit Price	Total Sales	Cost per Lot	Total Costs			
Group 1								
Group 2								
Group 3								
Schedule of								
Net Income								

Sullivan Furniture Company

Exercise 9-9

George Foreman Company

Section

Date   **Gene Tunney Company**

		1	2
(a)			
(b)			
(c)			

		1	2

Exercise 9-12

Floyd Patterson Company

(a)

(b)

Section ____

Date ____   **John Queensberry**

Exercise 9-14

Sugar Ray Company

Trampolines Inc.

			1	2

Becker Lumber Company

		Lumber	Millwork	Hardware

Aggassi Corporation

			1	2
(1)				
(2)				
(3)				
(4)				

Name

Section

Date   **Jimmy Conners Company**

		1	2
		Cost	Retail
(a)			
(b)			
(c)			
(d)			
(e)			
(f)			

Chris Evert Company

			1	2	3
			Cost		Retail

Section

Date   **Lendl's Boutique**

			1		2		3
			Cost				Retail

Helen Wills Company

			1	2
			Cost	Retail
(1)	Conventional Retail Method			
(2)	LIFO Retail Method			

			1	2
			Cost	Retail
(1)				
(2)				

(1)

(2)

Section

Date   **Red Barber Corporation**

(a)		1 Cost	2 Retail
(b)			
(c)			

DiMaggio Corporation

			1	2
1994				
1995				
1996				
1997				

Pete Company

	Item	1 Cost	2 Replacement Cost	3 Ceiling	4 Floor	5 Designated Market	6 Lower of Cost or Market

Section

Date

Lombardi Home Improvement Company

		1	2	3	4	5
(a)	Item	Cost	Replacement Cost	Ceiling	Floor	Lower of Cost or Market

(b)

Section

Date   **Puebla Corporation**

	1	2	3	4

(a)

(b)

Computations:

Revised income statements	1993	1994	1995	1996

(a)

(b)

J. Weissmuller Company

J. Weissmuller Company

(c)

Edmund Hillary Company

			1	2
(a)				
(b)				

			1		2

(a)	**Jim Thorpe Corporation**		1		2	
	Computation of Gross Profit Ratio					
	For the Eleven Months Ended May 31, 1996					

(b)	Computation of Cost of Goods Sold During June 1996

Jim Thorpe Corporation

			1	2
(c)	Computation of Inventory at June 30, 1996 By the Gross Profit Method			

			1	2	3	4
		Flojo Corporation Computation of Inventory Fire Loss April 15, 1996				

Computation of Gross Profit Margin

Problem 9-9

Albert Spalding's Discount Store

			1	2	3	4
1.						
2.						

Name

Section

Date

Yamaguchi Inc.

		1	2	3	4

Name

Section

Date

		1	2	3	4
(a)					
(b)					

		1	2
(a)			

		1	2	3	4
Continued					

(b)

(c)

Section

Date   **Unser Inc.**

	1	2	3	4
(a)				
(b)				

Name

Section

Date

Sprint Department Stores

(a)

(b)

		1	2	3 Cost	4 Retail

Name

Section

Date

Sprint Department Stores

(c)

(d)

Aquarius Shoppe

		1	2
(a)		Cost	Retail

(b)

(c)			1 Cost	2 Retail

Name

Section

Date

Bett's Stores Inc.

		1	2	3	4
(a)	Inventory Based on Conventional Retail Method				
(b)	Inventory Based on LIFO Retail Method				

Name

Section

Date

Shoreline Department Store

		1	2	3	4
(a)	Inventory Based on Conventional Retail Method				

(b)

Name

Section

Date

Shoreline Department Store

		1	2	3	4
(c)	Inventory Based on Dollar-Value LIFO Method				

(a)

(b)

(c)

(d)

Name

Section

Date

Name

Section

Date

		Item	1 Land	2 Land Improvements	3 Building	4 Other Accounts

Exercise 10-2

Paton Co.

				Land	Building

Section

Date   **McArthur Corporation**

			1		2	

Exercise 10-4

Montgomery Co.

			1		2	
Purchase						

		1	2	3	4

Construction

Exercise 10-5

Rommel Supply Company

		Land	Building	M & E	Other

				1		2

Accardo Furniture Company

(a)

(b)

Jared Jones Inc.

(a)

(b) | General Journal | Debit | Credit |

Jared Jones Inc.

(a)

(b)	General Journal		Debit	Credit

Situation I

Situation II

Situation III

Section ___________________________________

Date ___________________________________ **Allegro Engineering Corporation**

		General Journal		Debit	Credit
(a)					
(b)					
(c)					

Name

Section

Date

Andante Company

			1	2
	General Journal		Debit	Credit
(a)				
(b)				
(c)				

Vivace Company

1.				
2.				
3.				

Section

Date

Sebastian Bach, Inc.

			General Journal			1 Debit	2 Credit
(a)							
(b)							
(c)							
(d)							

Name

Section

Date

Hollerith, Inc.

		1	2
	General Journal	Debit	Credit
(a)			
(b)			
(c)			
	Schedule of Interest Amortization:		

Imelda Corporation and Capek Business Machine Company

General Journal		Debit	Credit
		1	2
Imelda Corporation			
Capek Business Machine Company			

Name

Section

Date

Dupré Company

(1)	General Journal		Debit	Credit

(2)				

		General Journal		1 Debit	2 Credit
		Dvořák Co.			
		Franz Liszt Co.			

Exercise 10-19

Beethoven Inc.

				1	2
(a)					

Beethoven Inc.

	General Journal	Debit	Credit
(b)			

Exercise 10-20

Elgar Resources Group

		General Journal		Debit	Credit
				1	2

Exercise 10-22

Name

Section

Date   **Grieg Inc.**

		1	2
	General Journal	Debit	Credit
(a)			
(b)			
(c)			

Exercise 10-24

Joplin Company

		General Journal		Debit	Credit

Exercise 10-25

Chopin Inc.

Name

Section

Date

Brahms Company

			1	2
(a)				
(b)				

Stefano DiMera Company

(a)

Analysis of Land Account for 1995

Analysis of Buildings Account for 1995

Analysis of Leasehold Improvements Account for 1995

		1	2
	Analysis of Machinery and Equipment Account for 1995		

(b)

John Black Corporation

(a)

Analysis of Land Account for 1995

Analysis of Land Improvements Account for 1995

Analysis of Buildings Account for 1995

Analysis of Machinery and Equipment Account for 1995

(a) Continued

Computation space for part a

(b)

Supporting Computations for part b

Section ___________________________

Date ___________________________ **Deveraux Company**

	General Journal		1 Debit	2 Credit
(a)				

Computation space for part a

Deveraux Company

			1	2
(b)				

Additional Computation space

Abe Carver Company

		General Journal		1 Debit	2 Credit

		1	2
(a)	Cost of Land		
(b)	Cost of Building		
	Schedule of Interest Capitalization		

Studebaker Corporation

			1	2
1.				
2.				

Section

Date

Studebaker Corporation

		1	2
3.			
4.			

Name

Section

Date

Chrysler, Inc. and Belvidere, Inc.

	General Journal		Debit	Credit
(a)				

Section

Date **Chrysler, Inc. and Belvidere, Inc.**

		General Journal		1 Debit	2 Credit
(b)					

Section _______________________________________

Date _______________________________________ **BelAir Construction and Impala Mfg. Co.**

		General Journal		Debit	Credit
(a)	1.				
	2.				
(b)	1.				
	2.				

Name

Section

Date

BelAir Construction and Impala Mfg. Co.

		General Journal		1 Debit	2 Credit
(c)	1.				
	2.				
(d)	1.				
	2.				

		1	2
(a)	Schedule of Self-Constructed Equipment Cost Stated at Full Cost		

Section

Date   **Bronco Mining Co.**

		1	2
(b)	Schedule of Self-Constructed Equipment Cost Stated at Incremental Cost		

(c)

(a)

(b) Transaction 1:

Transaction 2:

Pavlova Company

Transaction 3:

(c)

Pavlova Company

(a)

(b)

Name

Section

Date

Name

Section

Date

Name

Section

Date

Patsy Cline Company

(a)

(b)

(c)

Exercise 11-2

Everly Brothers Company

(a)

(b)

(c)

(d)

(e)

(f)

Exercise 11-3

LaVern Baker Company

(a)

(b)

Name

Section

Date

Skeeter Davis Furnace Corp.

(a)

(b)

(c)

(d)

(e)

(1)

(2)

(3)

(4)

Name

Section

Ben E. King Winery Company

Date

(a)

(b)

(c)

(d)

(e)

Five Satins Company

Exercise 11-8

Connie Francis Corporation

Section

Date **Marcy Walker Manufacturing Corporation**

(a)	Asset	1 Cost	2 Estimated Scrap	3 Depreciable Cost	4 Estimated Life	5 Depreciation per Year	6

(b)

(c)

Exercise 11-10

Side Kicks Co.

		Debit	Credit
(a)			
(b)			

Section

Date   **Alan Alda Company**

	General Journal		1 Debit	2 Credit

Exercise 11-12

Wayne Rodgers Company

	General Journal		Debit	Credit

Alistair Cooke Co.

	1	2
(a)		
(b)		

Exercise 11-14

Angela Lansbury Company

	1	2
(a)		
(b)		
(c)		
(d)		

		General Journal		1 Debit	2 Credit
(a)					
(b)					
(c)					
(d)					

		General Journal		1 Debit	2 Credit
(a)					
(b)		Computations:			
		1. Straight-line			
		2. Sum-of-the-years'-digits			

			1	2	3	4
				1990-1995		
			1989	Incl.	1996	Total
(a)	1.					
	2.					
	3.					
	4.					
	5.					
	6.					
(b)						

Fernandez Company

			1	2
(a)				
(b)				
(c)				

Section

Date **Fernandez Company**

			1	2
(a)				
(b)				
(c)				

Trassic Inc.

		1	2
(a)			
(b)			
(c)			
(d)			

Section

Date

Paleozoic Enterprises

		1	2
		1996	1997

(a)

(b)

(c)

(d)

Exercise 11-22

Pliocene Inc.

(a)

(b)

(c)

Kate Lockard Timber Company

(a)

(b)

Exercise 11-24

Marin Bosley Drilling Company

Paul Wenger Lumber Company

(a)

(b)

(c)

Exercise 11-26

Carrie Mosiman Mining Company

Paul Wenger Lumber Company

Section

(1)

(2)

			1	2
(a)	1.			
	2.			
	3.			
(b)				

			1 Depreciation Expense 1995	2 1996
1.	Straight-line			
2.	Units-of-output			
3.	Working Hours			
4.	Sum-of-the-years'-digits			
5.	Declining Balance			

(a)

1. Straight-line

2. Double-declining Balance:

3. Sum-of-the-years'-digits:

Vanessa Williams Company

(a)   4. Units-of-output:

(b)

		General Journal			Debit	Credit
(a)						

Name

Section

Date

Red Hot Tool Company

			1	2
(b)				

	General Journal		1 Debit	2 Credit
(a)				
(b)				
(c)				
(d)				
(e)				

LaShon Baily Mfg. Company

		1	2	3	4
(b)					

Splinter Logging and Lumber Company

(a)

(b)

(c)

(1)

(2)

(3)

(4)

(5)

(6)

(7)

Section

Date

Dorothea Dix Corporation

(8)

(9)

(10)

(11)

(12)

(13)

(14)

Section

Date   **Jose Amaro Corporation**

	General Journal		Debit	Credit
(1)				
(2)				

Section ___________________________

Date ___________________________ **Jose Amaro Corporation**

		General Journal			Debit	Credit
(3)						
(4)						
(5)						
(6)						

Section

Date

(a)   1. Straight-line Method

     2. Activity Method

     3. Sum-of-the-years'-digits Method

     4. Double-declining Balance Method

(b)   1. Straight-line Method

(b)   2. Sum-of-the-years'-digits Method

3. Double-declining Balance Method

Name

Section

Date

Name

Section

Date

Name

Section

Date

(a) (List by number)

(b)

(a)

(b)

Exercise 12-4

Arawak Company

1.

2.

3.

Section ____

Date ____ **Pequot Corporation**

	General Journal		1 Debit	2 Credit

Computations:

Wyandot Company

		General Journal		1 Debit	2 Credit
		Balance of Intangible Assets as of			
		December 31, 1996			
		Additional Computations:			

Drastic Plastic Corporation

(a)

(b)

Exercise 12-8

Narragansett Inc.

(a)

(b)

General Journal	Debit	Credit

Erie Corporation

		Inuit Company Intangibles Section of Balance Sheet December 31, 1996		1	2
		Computations:			

		Inuit Company Income Statement Effect For the Year Ended December 31, 1996		1	2

Section

Date   **Pueblo Inc.**

(a) Date	Description	1 Cost	2 Years to Run	3 Amortization per Year	4 Years to 12/31/95	5 6 Total Amortization to 12/31/95

(b)

Yakima Corporation

	(a) General Journal		1 Debit	2 Credit
(a)				
(b)				

Mohave Corporation

	General Journal	Debit	Credit
(a)			

Exercise 12-14

Who Company

		Debit	Credit
(a)			
(b)			
(c)			

Nuc-Air Division

		1	2
(a)			
(b)			

		1	2
(a)			
(b)	General Journal	Debit	Credit
(c)			
(d)			

Winnebago Company

Exercise 12-18

Crow Company

Winnebago Company

1.

2.

3.

4.

Exercise 12-20

Scioto Inc.

(a)

(b)

Section

Date   **Olentangy Enterprises**

	General Journal		Debit	Credit
(a)				
(b)				
(c)				
(d)				
(e)				

Section

Date   **Ojibwa Company**

			1	2

Sahaptin Petroleum Corporation

			1	2

Exercise 12-24

Algonquin News Inc.

Chippewa Records Corp.

Exercise 12-26

Menominee Company

(a)

(b)

Exercise 12-27

Comanche Corporation

(a)

(b)

(a)

(b)

Exercise 12-29

Kishwaukee Company

Section

Date   **Colin Davis Co.**

		General Journal			1 Debit	2 Credit

Eric Leinsdorf Laboratories

		1	2
(a)			
(b)			
(c)			

(a)

			1 Debit	2 Credit

Problem 12-3, Concluded

George Solti Corporation

			1	2
(b)				

Section

Date   **Inventa Product Company**

		1	2
(a)			
(b)	General Journal	Debit	Credit
(c)			
(d)			

(a)

(b)

(c)	General Journal	Debit	Credit

Joffrey Tool Company

(a)

(b)

		Adjusting Entries (not required) General Journal		1 Debit	2 Credit
1.					
2.					
3.					
4.					
5.					
6.					

Sara Cheng Corporation

			1	2
	Adjusting Entries (not required) General Journal		Debit	Credit
7.				
8.				
9.				

(a)

(b)

(c)

(d)

Section ____

Date ____ **Fritz Reiner Company**

		1	2

(a)

(b)

(a)

(b)

(c)

General Journal	Debit	Credit

André Previn Inc.

Financial Reporting Problem

Georgia-Pacific Corporation

1.

2.

Name

Section

Date

Name

Section

Date

Name

Section

Date

Exercise 13-2

Alpha Romero Corporation

General Journal	Debit	Credit
(a)		

Name

Section

Date

Alpha Romero Corporation

		General Journal		Debit	Credit
(b)					
(c)	(1)				
	(2)				

Exercise 13-3

Campari Company

Campari Company

Partial Balance Sheet

December 31, 1995

Note 1

			1	2
		Austin Healy Company		
		Partial Balance Sheet		
		December 31, 1995		
		Note 1		

Exercise 13-5

Mercer Company

			1	2
(a)		1994		
		1995		

(b)

Computations: parts a and b

Section

Date   **Mercer Company**

		General Journal		1 Debit	2 Credit
(a)		1994			
		1995			
(b)					

			1		2
			Debit		Credit

Exercise 13-8

Bently Company

			Debit		Credit

Section ____

Date ____ **Triumph Hardware Company**

		1 Total	2 Factory	3 Selling	4 Administrative
(a)					
	Wages				
	F.I.C.A.				
	Federal U.C.				
	State U.C.				
	Total Cost				
(b)	Factory Payroll:			Debit	Credit
	Sales Payroll:				
	Administrative Payroll:				

			1	2
			Debit	Credit
(a)				
(b)				

Name

Section

Date

Delage Equipment Company

		General Journal		1 Debit	2 Credit
(a)					
(b)					

Vauxhall Company

		General Journal		1 Debit	2 Credit
(a)					
(b)					
(c)					

	General Journal		1 Debit	2 Credit

Exercise 13-14

1.

2.

3.

Section

Date

			1	2
1.				
2.				
3.				

#	Assets	Liabilities	Owners' Equity	Net Income

(a)

(b)

(c)		Debit	Credit

Section

Date   **Duesenberg Company**

Duesenberg Company

Income Statement

For the Year 1995

Computation of Bonus and Tax

Section

Date   **Shao Yu Corporation**

		General Journal			1 Debit		2 Credit
(a)							

Name

Section

Date

Shao Yu Corporation

		General Journal		1 Debit	2 Credit
(b)					

		General Journal		1 Debit	2 Credit

		General Journal		1 Debit	2 Credit

		General Journal			1 Debit		2 Credit	

Section ____

Date _______________________________________ **Hasselback Import Company**

(a)	Name	1 Earnings To Aug. 31	2 Sept. Earnings	3 Income Tax With.	4 FICA	5 State U.C.	6 Federal U.C.
	J. Icerman						
	W. Heck						
	K. Lorek						
	T. Schaefer						
	S. Baginski						
	A. Nichols						
	Totals						

	General Journal		Debit	Credit
(b)				
(c)				

		1	2
(a)			
(b)			
(c)			
(d)			
(e)			
(f)			

Mind Benders Company

		General Journal		Debit	Credit
				1	2
(a)					
(b)					
(c)					
(d)					

Section

Date   **Willie Dixon Company**

		General Journal		1 Debit	2 Credit
(a)					
(b)					

(c)

(d)

		General Journal		1 Debit	2 Credit

Name

Section

Date

Yummy Candy Company

		General Journal			Debit		Credit
(a)		1995					
		1996					

		General Journal		1 Debit	2 Credit

(b)		Account	Classification	Amount 1995	1996

(a)

(b)

Ruby Lillian Corporation

(a)

(b)

    (1)

    (2)

    (3)

Name

Section

Date

Charlie Parker's Music Emporium

			1	2
1.				
2.				
3.				
4.				
5.				

(a)

(b)

(c)

(d)

Name

Section

Date

Jann Wenner Company

1.

2.

3.

Jann Wenner Company

1.

2.

3.

Georgia-Pacific Corporation

Name

Section

Date

Name

Section

Date

Name ________________________________

Section ________________________________

Date ________________________________   **Enrico Caruso Inc.**

Exercise 14-2

Section

Date   **Carmen Co. and Bizet Co.**

	General Journal		Debit	Credit
1.	Carmen Company			
2.	Bizet Company			

Maria Callas Company

		General Journal			1 Debit		2 Credit	
(a)								
(b)								

			1	2
(a)				
(b)				
(c)				

		General Journal			Debit	Credit
(a)	1.					
	2.					
	3.					
	4.					
(b)						

Section

Date

Beverly Sills Company

			1	2
(c)	1.			
	2.			
	3.			
	4.			

Section

Date   **Rossini Company**

	General Journal	Debit (1)	Credit (2)
(a)			

(b) Schedule of Interest Expense and Bond Amortization

Date	Credit Cash	Debit Interest Expense	Debit Bond Premium	Carrying Value of Bond

(c)

(d)

Name

Section

Date

Puccini Company

	General Journal		Debit (1)	Credit (2)

			1		2		3	
			Unsecured Bonds		Zero-Coupon Bonds		Mortgage Bonds	
(1)								
(2)								
(3)								
(4)								
(5)								
(6)								
	Computations:							

Tosca Corporation

	1	2

General Journal | Debit | Credit

		General Journal		1 Debit	2 Credit

Exercise 14-12

Aida Company

		General Journal		Debit	Credit
(a)					

Name

Section

Date

Aida Company

	General Journal		Debit	Credit
(b)			1	2

Exercise 14-13

Verdi Company

Traviata Company

		General Journal		1 Debit	2 Credit

Exercise 14-15

Rigoletto Company

		General Journal		Debit	Credit
(a)	1.				
	2.				
(b)	1.				
	2.				

		General Journal			1 Debit	2 Credit
(a)						
(b)						

Exercise 14-17

Lohengrin Co.

					1	2
(a)						
(b)						

Exercise 14-18

Seville Company

Exercise 14-19

Lalo Company

Name

Section

Date

American Store Company

	General Journal	1 Debit	2 Credit
(a)			
(b)			
(c)			

	1	2

(a)

(b)

(c) Interest Payment

Schedule After Debt Restructuring Date	Cash Interest	Effective Interest	Reduction of Carrying Amount	Carrying Amount of Note

(d)

(e)

			1	2
(a)				
(b)				

(c)	Interest Payment Schedule After Debt Restructuring	Date	Cash Interest	Effective Interest	Reduction of Carrying Amount	Carrying Amount of Note

(d)				
(e)				

Section

Date   **Robinson Company**

		1	2
(a)			
(b)			
(c)			

(d) Interest Payment Schedule After Debt Restructuring	Date	Cash Interest	Effective Interest	Reduction of Carrying Amount	Carrying Amount of Note
(e)					
(f)					

				1	2
(a)					
(b)	Interest Receipt				
	Schedule After				
	Debt Restructuring	Cash Interest	Effective Interest	Increase in Carrying Amount	Carrying Amount of Note
	Date				
(c)					
(d)					

		1	2
	General Journal	Debit	Credit
(a)	Toshiba Co:		
	Zimmer Inc.:		

Exercise 14-26

Eaton Corp. and First Trust

		1	2
(a)	1995:		
	1996:		
	1997:		

Eaton Corp. and First Trust Co.

		General Journal		Debit	Credit
(b)		1995			
		1996			
		1997			

Section

Date   **Eaton Corp. and First Trust**

		General Journal		Debit	Credit
(b)		1995			
		1996			
		1997			

		1	2
(a)			

(b)	Note Amortization Schedule	Date	Cash Received	Interest Revenue	Discount Amortized	Carrying Amount of Note

| (c) | | | |

	1	2

(a)

(c)   Note

Amortization Schedule	Cash Received	Interest Revenue	Discount Amortized	Carrying Amount of Note
Date				

(c)

		1	2

(a)

(b)

(c)

		General Journal		Debit	Credit
(d)					
(e)					
(f)					

Corvair Company

		1	2	3	4
Schedule of Discount Amortization Straight-line Method					
	Year	Credit Interest Payable	Debit Interest Expense	Credit Bond Discount	Carrying Value of Bonds

(b) Computation of the effective interest or yield rate

		1	2	3	4
Schedule of Discount Amortization Effective Interest Method					
	Year	Credit Interest Payable	Debit Interest Expense	Credit Bond Discount	Carrying Value of Bonds

Section

Date   **Riviera Co.**

	General Journal		1 Debit	2 Credit
	PLAN 1			
(a)				
(b)				
(c)				
	PLAN 2			
(a)				
(b)				
(c)				

Eldorado Company

		General Journal			1 Debit	2 Credit
(a)						
(b)						

	1	2	3	4

1. Brougham Co.

Computation of Discount on Bonds Payable:

Schedule of Bond Discount Amortization

Effective Interest Method

10% Bonds Sold to Yield 12%

Date	Cash Credit	Interest Expense Debit	Bond Discount Credit	Carrying Value of Bonds

General Journal			Debit	Credit

Brougham Co. and Biarritz Co.

		1 General Journal	2	3 Debit	4 Credit
1.	Continued				

2. **Biarritz Co.**

Computation of Premium on Bonds Payable

Schedule of Bond Premium Amortization

Effective Interest Method

12% Bonds Sold to Yield 10%

Date	Cash Credit	Interest Expense Debit	Bond Premium Debit	Carrying Value of Bonds

			1	2
	General Journal		Debit	Credit
2.	Continued			

		General Journal		1 Debit	2 Credit
2.		Continued			

		General Journal			1 Debit	2 Credit

Name

Section

Date

FleetLine Powerglide Corporation

		General Journal		Debit 1	Credit 2

	General Journal		Debit	Credit
(a)				
(b)				
(c)				
(d)				

Name

Section

Date

Impala Company

		General Journal		Debit	Credit
				1	2
(d)		(Continued)			

		1	2
(a)			
(b)			
(c)	General Journal	Debit	Credit
(d)			
(e)			
(f)			

Name

Section

Date

Malibu Co.

			1	2
(g)				

		1	2
	General Journal	Debit	Credit
(a)			

Name

Section

Date

Crosley Hotshot Company

		General Journal		1 Debit	2 Credit
(b)					
(c)					

(a)	Account Titles	1 Debit	2 Credit	3 4 Classification in Financial Statements
		December 31, 1994		
(b)		December 31, 1995		

Name

Section

Date **Falcon Company**

		General Journal		1 Debit	2 Credit
(a)					
(b)					
		Schedule of Note Discount Amortization			
(c)					

		General Journal		1 Debit	2 Credit
(a)					
(b)					
		Schedule of Note Discount Amortization			
(c)					

Name

Section

Date

Electia Cosmetics Co.

		General Journal			Debit	Credit
(d)						
(e)						

Name

Section

Date

(a)

(b)

(c)

(d)

(e)

			1	2
	DeVille Inc. Balance Sheet — Liability Section As of March 31, 1996			

Notes to Financial Statements

		1	2

(a)

(b) Schedule for Interest and Amortization

	Date	Cash Interest	Effective Interest	Discount Amortized	Carrying Amount

(e) Schedule for Intereest and Discount Aftger Debt Impairment Amortization

	Date	Cash Interest	Effective Interest	Discount Amortized	Carrying Amount

Ashland Company

1   2

(c)

(d)

(f)

Covaleski Inc.

	1	2

(a)

(b)

(c)

			1 Debit	2 Credit
(a)				
(b)				

Section ___________________________

Date ___________________________ **Downunder Corporation and Second National Bank**

		1	2
		Debit	Credit
(c)			
(d)			

Name

Section

Date

New York Inc. and Parsons Bank

		General Journal		1 Debit	2 Credit
(a)		Entries by New York Inc.:			
(b)		Entries by Parsons Bank:			

Section

Date   **Menlow Manufacturing Company and Janesville National Bank**

		General Journal		1 Debit	2 Credit
(a)					
(b)					

Crooch Corp. and Jenkins Corp.

(a)

Schedule of Debt Reduction and Interest Expense Amortization

(b)

Section

Date   **Crooch Corp. and Jenkins Corp.**

		1	2
(c)	Entries of Crooch Corp.:		
(d)	Entries of Jenkins Corp.:		

Georgia-Pacific Corporation

Name

Section

Date